D1196746

MICHAEL FARADAY

MARY ELIZABETH SALZMANN

Consulting Editor, Diane Craig, M.A./Reading Specialist

Super Sandcastle

An Imprint of Abdo Publishing
abdopublishing.com

abdopublishing.com

Published by Abdo Publishing, a division of ABDO, PO Box 398166, Minneapolis, Minnesota 55439. Copyright © 2017 by Abdo Consulting Group, Inc. International copyrights reserved in all countries. No part of this book may be reproduced in any form without written permission from the publisher. Super SandCastle™ is a trademark and logo of Abdo Publishing.

Printed in the United States of America, North Mankato, Minnesota
062016
092016

Editor: Rebecca Felix
Content Developer: Nancy Tuminelly
Cover and Interior Design and Production: Mighty Media, Inc.
Photo Credits: Shutterstock; Wellcome Library, London; Wikimedia Commons

Library of Congress Cataloging-in-Publication Data
Names: Salzmann, Mary Elizabeth, 1968- author.
Title: Michael Faraday / by Mary Elizabeth Salzmann ; consulting editor,
   Diane Craig, M.A./Reading Specialist.
Description: Minneapolis, Minnesota : Abdo Publishing, [2017] | Series:
   Scientists at work
Identifiers: LCCN 2015050526 (print) | LCCN 2016002517 (ebook) | ISBN
   9781680781564 (print) | ISBN 9781680775990 (ebook)
Subjects: LCSH: Faraday, Michael, 1791-1867--Juvenile literature. |
   Physicists--Great Britain--Biography--Juvenile literature.
Classification: LCC QC16.F2 S25 2017 (print) | LCC QC16.F2 (ebook) | DDC
   530/.092--dc23
LC record available at http://lccn.loc.gov/2015050526

Super SandCastle™ books are created by a team of professional educators, reading specialists, and content developers around five essential components—phonemic awareness, phonics, vocabulary, text comprehension, and fluency—to assist young readers as they develop reading skills and strategies and increase their general knowledge. All books are written, reviewed, and leveled for guided reading, early reading intervention, and Accelerated Reader™ programs for use in shared, guided, and independent reading and writing activities to support a balanced approach to literacy instruction.

CONTENTS

A FAMOUS SCIENTIST

Michael Faraday was a scientist. He made many discoveries. He is known for his work with electricity and magnets.

Michael Faraday invented many scientific devices.

MICHAEL FARADAY

BORN: September 22, 1791, Newington Butts, England

MARRIED: Sarah Barnard, June 12, 1821

CHILDREN: none

DIED: August 25, 1867, Middlesex, England

A HARD START

Michael grew up near London, England. He had three **siblings**. His father was a blacksmith. The family did not have much money.

Michael learned to read and write. But he did not go to school very long. School cost money. His family could not afford it.

London, England

FIRST JOB

Michael began working at age 13. He **delivered** newspapers. He worked for George Riebau. Riebau also bound and sold books. He taught Michael to bind books.

Michael read the books he bound. He kept learning! Michael liked science books best.

EARLY EXPERIMENTS

Faraday took notes as he read. He did experiments too. He built a **generator**. He also made an early type of **battery**.

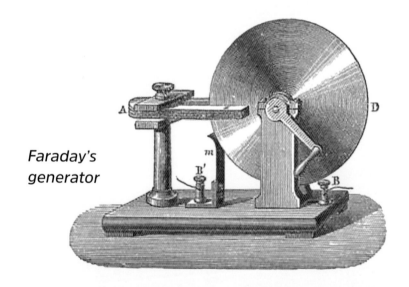

Faraday's generator

An early battery

CHEMISTRY

In 1812, Faraday heard
Humphry Davy speak.
Davy was a chemist.
He taught at the Royal
Institution. It is in
London.

Humphry Davy

After the **lecture**, Faraday wrote Davy a letter. He asked Davy for a job.

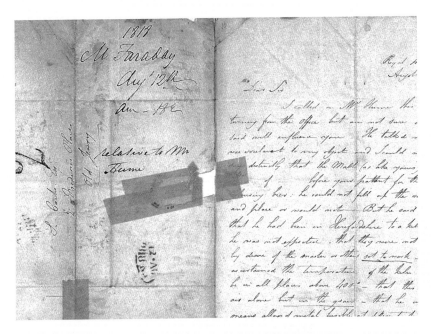

A letter Faraday wrote to Davy in 1819

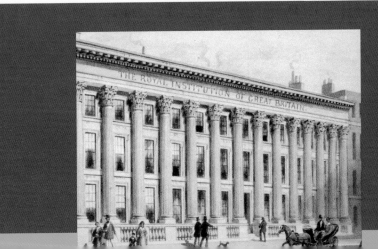

Davy hired him in 1813. Faraday worked for Davy until 1820.

The Royal Institution

ON HIS OWN

Faraday stayed at the Royal Institution. But now he worked on his own. He did his own experiments. He became a well-known chemist.

Faraday did many experiments with electricity.

Faraday discovered benzene in 1825. Benzene is a chemical. It is used in gasoline. He also worked with steel and glass. He tried to create better glass for telescope lenses.

People use telescopes to see faraway objects, such as stars.

MAKING A MOTOR

Faraday studied **electromagnetism**. Scientists thought it could be used to make a motor. Many tried to build one. Faraday did too. His was the first motor that worked!

Hans Christian Ørsted was another scientist who worked with electromagnetism.

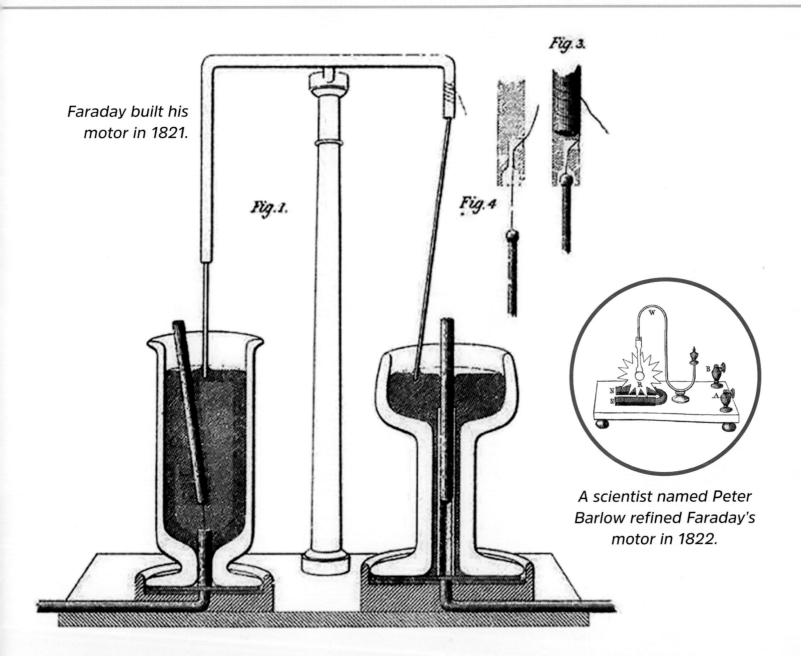

Faraday built his motor in 1821.

Fig. 1.

Fig. 3.

Fig. 4

A scientist named Peter Barlow refined Faraday's motor in 1822.

MORE EXPERIMENTS

Faraday did a new experiment in 1831. He used a **battery** and a magnetic ring. He also used two wires.

Electric current flowed through one wire. It passed through the ring. It flowed to the other wire. This is **electromagnetic** induction. It is Faraday's most famous discovery.

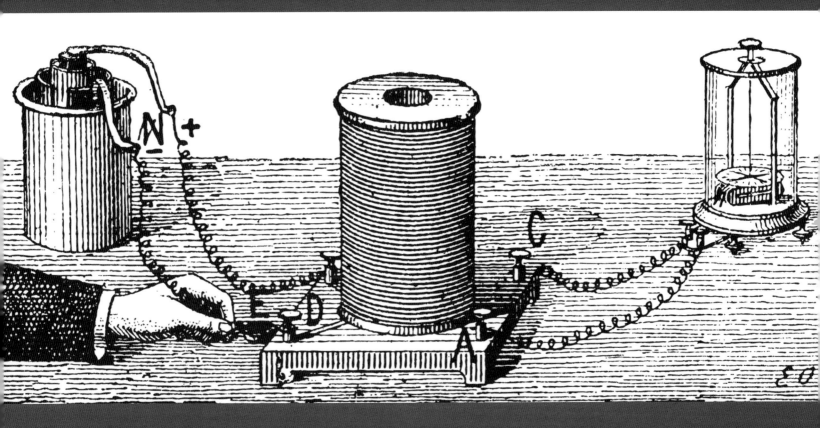

LATER LIFE

Faraday studied science all his life. He was also a teacher. He gave **lectures**. He wrote a book on chemistry.

Faraday became head of the laboratory at the Royal Institution in 1825.

Faraday retired in 1862. Queen Victoria gave him a house. It was a reward for his life's work. He lived there until he died in 1867.

Faraday wrote many notes and letters during his lifetime. Several are on display in museums.

MORE ABOUT FARADAY

Faraday made up many SCIENCE TERMS.

He was AGAINST WAR. He would not make weapons.

Faraday invented a BURNER. It was used in labs.

TEST YOUR KNOWLEDGE

1. What was Faraday's first job?

2. What chemical did Faraday discover in 1825?

3. Faraday built the first working motor. *True or false?*

THINK ABOUT IT!

Have you ever used a magnet? What did you use it for?

ANSWERS: 1. Delivering newspapers   2. Benzene   3. True

GLOSSARY

battery – a container filled with chemicals that makes electrical power.

deliver – to take something somewhere or to someone.

electromagnetism – magnetism created by a current of electricity.

generator – a machine that creates electricity.

lecture – a talk that is planned ahead of time and given to an audience or class.

sibling – a brother or sister.